WHERE IS GOD AMIDST THE BOMBS?

A PRIEST'S REFLECTIONS FROM THE COMBAT ZONE

C. Neal Goldsborough
Chaplain, U.S. Navy

cover design: ALBONETTI DESIGN
©2008 FORWARD MOVEMENT

Forward Movement
300 West Fourth Street, Cincinnati, Ohio 45202 USA
www.forwardmovement.org   1-800-543-1813

Contents

4

Foreword

Once in awhile we have an opportunity to enter a story before the headline is written, before the smoke drifts off the scene or reports of casualties are picked up by wire services. News accounts of war may linger briefly and then be forgotten, but the grinding human drama is played out by valiant men and women in a field hospital. It has always been that way but today there is a new kind of conflict. Technological advances have brought survival to soldiers who wouldn't have lived past the first hour in the last war. This is the place Neal Goldsborough reveals to us, and I am proud to say I know the priest behind these pages. He is the Naval Reserve chaplain who was a primary responder at the Pentagon on September 11, 2001. He was quick to be a sensitive pastor amid that chaos, so it shouldn't surprise us that he does the same when he is assigned to this clinic in southwest Asia. This time he brings us along.

As we go he invites us to live through the consequences with him. How does one experience the holy and divine in a lethal battle area which is so devastating that it shreds limb and soul? The reader should be prepared for this uncompromising and bracing narrative, for Neal's easy writing style is matched by a remarkable ability to see his surroundings as they set and summarize the tone of a moment. In one instance, before relating yet another human drama, he pauses to read the instructions over the ice machine in the morgue, "Scoops: 7, head; 5, chest; 10, legs."

In this bracing chronology of his tour of duty we meet men and women in the places where life holds on by a thin thread. Is life to be summed up by the physical reconstruction applied through the skill of talented surgeons? Chaplain Goldsborough gives such clinicians special credit, but he also keeps the story from any mere reduction as he intersperses the unrelenting carnage with his own reflections and a creative running dialogue with snatches from a book written by World War I Chaplain

Geoffrey Anketell Studdert Kennedy. Noting that this brother chaplain faced similar draining hospital duty, he says that both he and Studdert Kennedy "began to raise some difficult questions about life and death and evil and the existence of an all-powerful God of love." These asides serve as a buffer giving us a breather and moments for deeper reflection with both chaplains.

Courage is a unique and often quiet by-product of war. It is a precious commodity because it is an assurance that some of us are willing to take huge risks to be present with others in the uncertainty of the next moment. Neal Goldsborough, as a sensitive chronicler and survivor of such days, wears such a badge of recognition among us.

George E. Packard
Bishop Suffragan for Chaplaincies
February 2008

Woodbine Willie

His experience of war was vastly different from mine. The Western Front in 1916 saw unimaginable carnage. That summer, on one day, July 1, the first day of the Battle of the Somme, the British army suffered more than 57,000 casualties, including 20,000 dead or missing. The soldiers died to capture a few hundred yards of ground, and most failed to take their objectives. Into the muddy hell of those trenches stepped a most unlikely figure, Geoffrey Anketell Studdert Kennedy, a priest of the Church of England and a new chaplain in the British Army, who would eventually gain fame as "Woodbine Willie."

Described by one nurse as the ugliest man she had ever seen, with his long hound-dog face, protruding elephantine ears, and bullfrog's mouth, Studdert Kennedy's contemporaries also remembered his compassionate dark brown eyes that betrayed a touch of sadness. An absent-minded man who often wore his uniform incorrectly, he was frequently asked after the war to conduct marriage ceremonies for ex-officers. "If you mean Studdert Kennedy," said one cleric who was asked to let him officiate in his parish church, "I advise you to have someone in reserve. He will probably forget to turn up."

The troops loved him and gave him the nickname "Woodbine Willie" because of his habit of handing out packs of Woodbine cigarettes to the men in the trenches. One biographer said, "He shocked the conventional because he often played the fool for Christ's sake, giving himself to the needs of the men without a thought for any status, clerical or military."

When asked about the spiritual ministry of a chaplain he said, "There is very little; it's all muddled and mixed. Take a box [of cigarettes] in your haversack and a great deal of love in your heart, and go up to them: laugh with them, joke with them. You can pray *with* them sometimes; but pray *for* them always." His soldiers knew he cared for them because he shared fully in their danger and misery. And he had the courage to speak the truth to the powerful. Given the honor of preaching before King George V, he tossed aside his prepared text and began: "I come to you from the bloody slime of the trenches…"

A man of awesome physical courage, he was decorated with the Military Cross for bravery under fire at Messines Ridge in 1917. His unconventional Christianity and moral courage offended those who wanted simple answers to the complex moral questions raised by the war. General Sir Herbert Plumer, Commander of the Second Army, was so angered by one of Studdert Kennedy's sermons that he walked out of the service. Later, a fellow staff officer said, "Are you the fellow who preached this morning?"

"I have that honor," Studdert Kennedy replied.

"Well, all I can say is: you ought to be cashiered or locked up in an asylum."

Woodbine Willie, in his book *The Hardest Part,* accompanied me to my war.

The carnage in the Iraq war has not approached that of World War I. In Iraq in 2005, after two years of conflict, we had reached 2,000 dead. I never set foot in Iraq and I never had a shot fired at me. My wartime experiences were confined to a forty-four bed combat support hospital, Expeditionary Medical Facility Dallas, at Camp Arifjan, Kuwait, in direct support of the war effort.

Camp Arifjan was a vast staging arena for the "war up north" and most of the troops coming in and out of Iraq came through our camp. From January to March 2005 we witnessed the largest transfer of U.S. troops since World War II. Fully 150,000 came though Camp Arifjan on their way home, as an additional 150,000 arrived in theatre. Every day during those months over a thousand trucks headed north from Arifjan. Many of these soldiers, sailors, airmen, and marines came to our hospital, and a hospital was where both Studdert Kennedy and I began to raise questions about life and death and evil and the existence of an all-powerful God of love.

I had been in France as a chaplain about two months before I had heard a gun fired or seen a trench. I went to see an officer in a base hospital who was slowly recovering from very serious wounds. The conversation turned on religion and he seemed anxious to get at the truth. He asked me a tremendous question. "What I want to know, Padre," he said, "is what is God like? When I am transferred into a new battalion I want to know what the Colonel is like. He bosses the show, and it makes a lot of difference to me what sort he is. Now I realize that I am in the battalion of humanity, and I want to know what the Colonel of the world is like. That is your business, Padre. You ought to know."

When a chaplain joins a battalion no one says a word to him about God, but everyone asks him, in a thousand different ways, "What is God like?" His success or failure as a chaplain really depends on the answer he gives by word and by deed. The answer by deed is the more important, but an answer by words is inevitable and must be given somehow.

When the question was put to me in the hospital I pointed to a crucifix which hung over the officer's bed and said, "Yes, I think I can tell you. God is like that." I wondered if it would satisfy him. It did not.

He was silent for a while, looking at the crucifix, and then he turned to me, and his face was full of doubt and disappointment. "What do you mean? God cannot be like that. God is Almighty, Maker of heaven and earth, Monarch of the world, the King of kings and Lord of lords, whose will sways all the world. That is a battered, wounded, bleeding figure, nailed to a cross and helpless, defeated by the world and broken in all but spirit. That is not God; it is part of God's plan: God's mysterious, repulsive, and apparently perfectly futile plan for saving the world from sin. I cannot understand the plan, and it appears to be a thoroughly bad one, because it has not saved the world from sin. It has been an accomplished fact now for nearly two thousand years, and we have sung hymns about God's victory, and yet the world is full of sin and now there is this filthy war. I'm sick of this cant. You have not been up there, Padre, and you know nothing about it. I tell you that the cross does not help me a bit; it makes things worse. I admire Jesus of Nazareth; I think He was splendid, as my friends at the front are splendid—splendid in their courage, patience and unbroken spirit.

"But I asked you not what Jesus *was* like, but what God *is* like, God who willed His death in agony upon the Cross, and who apparently wills the wholesale slaughter in this war. Jesus

Christ I know and admire, but what is God
Almighty like? To me He is still the unknown
God."

How would you answer him?

This book is my answer to Chaplain Studdert
Kennedy's question. The questions war raises
about the loving and omnipotent God are the
same in every generation.

౼౼౼

A Note about Sources

Unless otherwise noted, the quotations indented and
set off from the text are from these works by G. A.
Studdert Kennedy:

The Hardest Part (London: Hodder and Stoughton,
1919).

The Unutterable Beauty (London: Hodder and Stoughton, 1927). This book is also the source of the poems
"Waste" and "At a Harvest Festival" (the text of Hymn
9 in *The Hymnal 1982*.)

The biographical information and the quote in the
introduction about Studdert Kennedy being "cashiered
or locked up" are from *Woodbine Willie* by William
Purcell (London: Hodder and Stoughton, 1962).

Chapter 1

The Saddest Room

*Now when the centurion, who stood facing him,
saw that in this way he breathed his last, he said,
"Truly this man was God's son."*

—Mark 15:39

The high-velocity bullet entered the twenty-seven-year-old sergeant's face below his left eye. It exited his head and blew away most of his skull from an inch above his eyebrows. By the time our casualty receiving team removed his body from the helicopter he had bled out all over the chopper's floor. They tried valiantly to get his breathing started, but everyone knew their efforts would be in vain. He was "called" at 1538 (3:38 p.m. local time) and I was called to his stretcher at the same time.

I took out my stole and oil stock and asked for quiet. A profound stillness now replaced the frenetic energy of the ward. I reached out with my thumb to mark his brow with the sign of the cross and realized that he no longer had a forehead, so I signed his good cheek with the mark of baptism. "Let us pray," I said, and the doctors, nurses, and corpsmen bowed their heads. Most touched him. One knelt on the bloody floor with his head touching the gurney. I was told the sergeant was Roman Catholic so I had brought one of the rosaries from my office. I placed it in his hands. Perhaps his parents would later treasure it as a priceless relic of their son's last moments. I said the commendation from *The Book of Common Prayer*: "Depart, O Christian soul, out of this world…May your rest be this day in peace, and your dwelling place in the Paradise of God." I concluded with the Hail Mary: "Holy Mary, Mother of God, pray for us sinners now and at the hour of our death," adding "Holy Mary, Mother of God, pray for your child now, at the hour of his death."

So Joseph took the body and wrapped it in a clean linen cloth.

—Matthew 27:59

After some silence, we began to clean up the makeshift clinic. Two corpsmen gently, almost tenderly, wiped the blood off his body. Others mopped his blood from the tent floor. I helped hold the body bag open as they carefully lifted him into its blackness. We curtained off an examination area in the room across the passageway as a quiet place where his body would rest until it could be transported to the morgue later that evening. I was concerned about our staff which had just been through an emotionally wrenching experience. After the cleanup, I commented to a young corpsman that this was difficult work. She agreed. I asked her if she, as a respiratory therapist, did this sort of thing in her civilian work. She said, "Yes, but this is harder because he died for someone else's country."

I asked one of the staff to find my chaplain's assistant, Petty Officer Bill Meyer. He arrived in a few minutes, and I asked him to call Camp Arifjan's Roman Catholic chaplain. The chaplain came quickly and Petty Officer Meyer, a devout Roman Catholic, assisted him in performing the rites of their church. I thanked the chaplain by saying that the sergeant's family would be comforted with the knowledge a Catholic priest had given him last rites.

It took several hours to complete arrangements to transport the soldier's body to the morgue. Petty Officer Meyer and I took turns keeping vigil with him. We made certain that he was never left alone until he was handed over to the mortuary staff. The crew of six on the ambulance was composed of Meyer, four of the corpsmen who had worked to save the sergeant's life, and me. It was important for them to experience some closure by carrying him on the next step of his journey home. It was dark when we left the hospital. The entire hospital staff stood silently at attention and saluted as we placed his body in the ambulance.

…and laid it in his own new tomb, which he had hewn in the rock. He then rolled a great stone to the door of the tomb and went away.

—Matthew 27:60

Every hospital keeps its morgue tucked in some remote corner of the building, far from the beaten path. One has to be very intentional about finding it. The army's morgue is no exception. It is at the far end of the airport down a winding alley behind several buildings. There is no sign on the outside of the building identifying it as the morgue, only a bright red sign that reads "Access Restricted." This could be any commercial building with a wooden loading platform in front of double doors. The only clue is the metal coffins stacked outside like upside-down aluminum fishing boats.

The Army's Mortuary Affairs department is staffed by a wonderful group of National Guardsmen from Puerto Rico. These dedicated men and women go about their grim work with solemn, compassionate dignity. They are among the unknown and unsung heroes of this war. As we wheeled the soldier's body through the doors we entered their world. It was the saddest room I've ever seen. The room is about twenty by twenty-four feet. The walls are eggshell white and there is an immaculately clean floor covered in fake brown wood parquet linoleum. On one wall hangs a huge American flag. On the wall perpendicular to it are two large ice machines with a sign over them that reads: "Scoops: 7 Head; 5 chest; 10 legs." Directly across the room hangs a white board that has written in a column: "234, CIV, followed by his name; 235, Sgt. _____, USMC; 236, decapitated portion." Along the same wall are stacked boxes and boxes of American flags. There is also a set of shelves made from two-by-fours holding dozens of large bottles of pine oil and other disinfectants.

The most heart-rending sight is in the middle of the floor. There in a ten-by-fifteen-foot area are neatly arranged footlockers, duffle bags and sea bags, backpacks, and cardboard boxes closed with gray duct tape. Each is secured with a red metal seal, and there is a sign taped on each one that bears the name of a soldier, his or her unit, and the word "deceased." These are the personal effects of the dead, waiting to be shipped home to wives or husbands, children or parents. One can only begin to imagine the pain and grief that arrive with these possessions.

We assisted the mortuary crew as they gently lifted the soldier's body into the GI-issue metal coffin. They unzipped the body bag, placed an ID tag on his wrist, and resealed the bag. They also taped a label to the inside of the casket lid. They closed the coffin and latched it shut.

As the flag was reverently placed on it, our senior chief called "attention" and we rendered honors: a salute. It was after midnight of a very long day.

The women who had come with him from Galilee followed, and they saw the tomb and how his body was laid. Then they returned…
—Luke 23:55-56

Outside, as we prepared to leave, one of the Mortuary Affairs' soldiers offered us some "Puerto Rican coffee." We were taken aback—and pleased—at this gracious hospitality. Petty Officer Meyer, a world-class coffee lover, was the only one to take them up on it. Someone asked if they had any Bacardi, and we all laughed at the thought in this "dry" Islamic country. More than a few of our group said they could use a drink. The simple act of their hospitality, however, moved us from sadness to a sense of gratitude for something as simple as a cup of coffee.

On the way home Petty Officer Meyer noticed I still had the sergeant's blood stains on my uniform. We spent the trip back to Camp Arifjan eating dry Frosted Flakes and

Girl Scout cookies in the darkness of the back of the ambulance, reflecting on the meaning of what we had done. And discussing the best method of laundering the dried blood from my shirt.

> I don't know or love the Almighty potentate—my only real God is the suffering Father revealed in the sorrow of Christ. How can a man believe in an absolute Almighty God? What's He doing? Could He be sleeping? God Himself seems non-existent—the Almighty Ruler whom all things obey. He seems to have gone to sleep and allowed all things to run amuck. I don't believe in an absolute Almighty Ruler. I don't see how anyone can believe it. If it were a choice between that God and no God, I would be an atheist. But how near the God Whom Christ revealed comes at a time like this: nearer than breathing, nearer than hands and feet, the Father of sorrow and love Who spoke through the crucified Son.

Chapter 2

Beauty Nearly Missed

Not here for high and holy things
We render thanks to Thee,
But for the common things of earth,
The purple pageantry
Of dawning and of dying days,
The splendor of the sea.

— #9, *Hymnal 1982*
G. A. Studdert Kennedy

Over here we live in a monochromatic world. The ground is sand. Sometimes, when there is a sandstorm, the air turns beige. We wear tan camouflage uniforms. Our hospital's tents are sand-colored.

One of the hardest adjustments on leaving this place, people say, is returning to a world of color. One friend who just came back from R&R said he had sat at his window for over an hour and just stared at the green grass and trees. He said it was like going from Kansas to Oz. The beauty of home was overwhelming after living in this dull, drab world for six months. He said he could even see the stars at night. We don't have stars here, because their light is overpowered by the brilliant glare of the searchlights surrounding our fortified perimeter. We rarely see or hear birds here, except sparrows. Kuwait is such a barren land that it has no indigenous species of birds.

Last week I was watching our hospital's softball team play a night game. As I sat in the bleachers I felt something creeping across my hand. Fearing it might be one of the ubiquitous scorpions, I slowly raised my arm and saw, of all things, a dragonfly. I've always been partial to those beautiful insects with their brilliantly jeweled, iridescent bodies. This one, sadly, was totally beige, the pale color of the desert sand. How tragic, I thought—even the dragonflies over here can't catch a break. They're ugly, too. Then I reconsidered. The bug had beige lace-like wings, delicately lovely in their own strange way. I had been too quick to judge what was different from my own experience;

I almost missed out on something profoundly beautiful.

Now I'm waging my own personal guerrilla war against this dull existence. I ordered a reproduction of a large Navy recruiting poster from 1919. It says: "Give the World the Once Over in the United States Navy." The poster's sailors are depicted in bold, primary colors having fun visiting exotic India. It is so bold that its color slaps you in the face as you walk past my office. There is a subversive side to it, too. One of our administrative petty officers picked up on it: "Sir, I like your poster, but the Navy has us stuck here in the desert for a year, and we cannot even leave this base. I've been here six months and I have yet to even meet a Kuwaiti, and the only liberty we get is through the windshield of a vehicle. Is that poster a joke?"

"Yes, Petty Officer Rodriguez!" I said, "You've caught the meaning of that poster that several admirals and generals have missed."

Chapter 3

I Believe in God
the Father, the Almighty?

Two weeks ago I was awakened early in the morning and called to the hospital for a "code," medical lingo for a death. A soldier had been out running and collapsed. He died in our casualty receiving ward (the equivalent of a civilian ER).

We didn't know who he was for nearly an hour. He had no identification on him, not even his dog tags. Yet he looked familiar to me. Someone said he might be the guy who leads the choir at one of the Sunday services, so we called an Army chaplain to help us identify him.

When the Army chaplain looked at the body he said, "Oh, my God! That's Chaplain Smith! Chaplain Smith is dead." Then I, too, recognized the chaplain who had been "in-country" only three weeks, and whom I'd met maybe two or three times. Word of this tragedy spread quickly, and the news left his unit in emotional shock and grief. His death also left some theological wreckage. "How could this happen?" many wanted to know. "If anyone was close to the Lord, it was Chaplain Smith."

Our soldiers, sailors, airmen and marines see their chaplains as many things: a reassuring presence, a compassionate counselor and confidant, an object of derision as a non-combatant in a "warrior" culture, a man or woman of God who reminds them that God is with them wherever they are, a moral judge, a detested symbol of organized religion for those burned by the church in the past, a harbinger of disease and death as one who brings Red Cross messages from loved ones at home, and finally a friend to all who treats everyone with the same dignity and respect, regardless of rank.

To most people, their chaplain is a good luck charm, especially in a combat zone. It may be superstitious, but I've heard it said more than once, "Thank God the chaplain's here—everything is gonna be OK!" So what happens if the chaplain dies?

What does this mean? Where is God in all this? What was God thinking to "take" him now? How could God let this happen to him and to us? And behind this question is the thought: If it could happen to him, then it could happen to me.

Many soldiers didn't know what to do with Chaplain Smith's untimely death. He left a wife, three grown children, and five grandchildren. More than a few soldiers still buy off on an immature, bankrupt theology that says if you love God and try to live by his rules, good things will happen to you, and if you don't, bad things will happen to you.

Others said, "It was God's will" or "The Lord took him" or "The Lord called him home" or other such horrible caricatures of a God who would inflict pain and grief on Chaplain Smith and on those who loved him. They were wrestling with what it means to have an all-powerful God who is also good and just and loving.

I remember this cosmic conundrum being described this way in seminary:

If God is good, then he is not omnipotent.
If God is omnipotent, then he is not good.

So, once again, I turned to my conversations with Studdert Kennedy, to see how he wrestled with this age-old issue. He struggled, too. In his book *The Hardest Part,* written in 1918, he writes:

God's helpless to prevent war or else He wills it and approves of it. There is the alternative. You pay your money and you take your choice. (Does God will war?) If you cling to God's absolute omnipotence, you must believe it. If God is absolutely omnipotent, He must will war, since war is and always has been the commonplace of history. Men are driven to the conclusion that war is the will of the Almighty God.

If it is true, I go morally mad. Good and evil cease to have any meaning. If anything is evil, war is. It is a cruel and insane waste of energy and life. If God wills war, then I am morally mad and life has no meaning. I hate war, and if God wills it I hate God, and I am a better man for hating Him. In that case the first and great commandment is, "Thou shalt hate the Lord thy God with all thy heart, and Him only shalt thou detest and despise."

Then I give up. I can't see God and I can't love Him. I turn back to Christ. I can see and love Him. He could not will war. He brought strife upon earth, because he roused the powers of evil by challenging them; but He did not will strife: He suffered agony and death because of it, and pleaded with men to conquer evil and learn to live in peace. ....If God does not suffer agony because of war, and if He does not will that men should live at peace, then I cannot and will not worship Him. I hate Him. This is not merely an intellectual alternative, it is a moral one. It lives and burns. It is a matter of life and death which side you take. If it were merely intellectual it would not matter.

The truth is that history drives one to the knowledge that God cannot be absolutely Almighty. God, the Father God of Love, is everywhere in history, but nowhere is He Almighty. Ever and always we see Him suffering, striving, crucified, but conquering. God is Love. ....

The Church has taught her children the conception of God as One who can do anything He likes whenever He likes, and the effort to square that concept with the facts is wrecking their faith.

Studdert Kennedy would have railed at a recent book by a Navy chaplain who served with the Marines in Iraq at the beginning of this war. Its author posits God answering the prayers of his Marines and saving them in combat time and again. Yet he cannot, and does not, attempt to explain God's action (or lack thereof) in the deaths of those killed in combat or in accidents.

Studdert Kennedy and I run from this simplistic, bizarre theology. He finally places the dilemma of the omnipotence of God on the cross. In the cross he finds

> The Truth that human sin and sorrow matter to God, nay, are matters of life and death to God, as they must be to me. In Him I find the truth that the moral struggle of man is a real struggle because God is in it, in it and beyond it too, for in the Risen Christ who conquered death and rose again I find the promise and guarantee that the moral struggle of the human race will issue in victory. In Him I still can stand and say my Creed from the bottom of my heart. For there is a sense in which I believe

more firmly than I ever did before that God is Almighty. And in those glorious words of the Creed I confess my faith that the final victory of God is as sure, nay, surer than the rising of tomorrow's sun. God is suffering His agony now, but the day will surely come when His agony and ours will be ended. Sin and sorrow, though real, are only temporary, the results of temporary necessities inherent in the task of creation, but they will pass away, and God will prove Himself Almighty in the end.

My friend, the chaplain from the First World War, would agree that "God earns the right to be God on the cross" and suffers still in his love for all creation. And that in the end all creation will share in the almighty power of Jesus' resurrection—including the late Chaplain Smith and all who have suffered and died in this terrible war. In the words of medieval English mystic Dame Julian of Norwich: "All will be well, and all will be well, and all manner of thing will be well."

Chapter 4

"All Who Exalt Themselves Will Be Humbled"

The military is a highly structured world of rules and regulations. That fact has not changed since Woodbine Willie's day. The clothes we wear are called uniforms for good reason—we all must look the same. A non-military friend of mine was amazed that the Navy could tell me what type of undershirt I could and could not wear with my khakis. And every service member at Camp Arifjan must obey the same general orders to ensure the efficient, safe, and disciplined function of this base. Except...

There are even rules governing who can eat at our "dining facility," the new name the Army gives to the mess or chow hall. These rules are posted outside the doors for all to see. All weapons must be cleared before you enter, so that no one has live ammo in the chamber. This makes sense. No one should worry about being shot accidentally during a meal. In addition, no bags of any kind are permitted inside, for security reasons. This includes briefcases, backpacks, rucksacks, even plastic bags with one's latest purchases from the PX. Everyone is also required to show a military ID card upon entering the chow line, even if he is in uniform. And finally, one must conform to a strict dress code, especially for civilian attire—no sleeveless shirts or blouses, no shorts or skirts above mid-thigh, no T-shirts with offensive slogans (whatever those are), no sandals or open-toed shoes, no sweaty gym clothes, no sunglasses hanging around your neck while in uniform, no shirts that expose the stomach, and so on. Everyone must conform, yet there are always people who feel the rules don't apply to them.

You know the type, the guy or gal with the Leona Helmsley sense of entitlement who thinks rules only apply to "little people." These folks believe that because of wealth, profession, standing in the community, education, or family connections they should not have to submit to tiresome things like waiting in line. These are the self-exalting people whom Jesus blasts, the people he says are farthest from the kingdom of God. Sadly we have more than a few of these in the military.

One of our sailors recently had lunchtime clicker duty at the dining facility. The clicker duty person stands at the door with a mechanical counter "clicking" the number of people who eat at the facility. He also checks ID cards and enforces the dress codes. This particular sailor is usually an upbeat person, but he was down in the dumps the day I came through the line. "What's up?" I asked. It seems that a few minutes before, a man in civilian clothes, carrying a PX shopping bag, had come through the line. The young sailor asked him for his ID and he said, "I don't have to show my ID card. I'm the base Command Sergeant Major."

The sailor replied that everyone had to show an ID. How else could he know that the man was who he said he was? The sergeant major raised his voice and pointed to his photograph on the wall of the vestibule of the dining hall. "That's me," he said. "Now don't you forget it."

The sailor then said, "Sergeant Major, everyone is required to show his military ID. And you are not permitted to bring that bag into the dining area." The sergeant major said, "I don't have to put up with this crap!" and pushed his way into the line. No one in the line came to the aid of the junior enlisted sailor, or called the sergeant major on his boorish conduct. All it took for this arrogant, self-important man to get away with flaunting the rules and abusing a "little person" was for everyone else to look the other way.

The sergeant major was an important person who had the ear of the commanding general and who could be a benefactor to anyone on base. No one wanted to challenge him because he might need something from him or the general some day.

I tried to offer support to the sailor, but it was too little, too late. I suggested the next time anyone with a bag pushed his way into the dining facility, even the sergeant major, he should immediately call the MPs to have the person escorted out. I told him I would support him if I was within earshot if it ever happened again.

I wondered if the sergeant major had forgotten, in his self-importance, what it was like to be that junior enlisted nobody who not only had to wait in line and obey the rules, but had to take the verbal and emotional abuse of those who thought they were above everyone else. I knew in this case which side Jesus was on.

Chapter 5

Memorial Day Flags

We had our third fatality several weeks ago. A private was unloading his armored personnel carrier from a ship. The tracked vehicle collided with a self-propelled howitzer and the barrel of the gun struck his head, smashing his skull and causing him to expel his brains out his nose and mouth. He had been in theatre five days. Our skilled casualty receiving team worked valiantly to resuscitate him, but he probably died instantly. I assisted the army's accident investigation agent by holding the dead man's hands while he was fingerprinted. Our youngest sailor, nicknamed "the Kid," age nineteen, was assigned to search through his blood-soaked, brain-splattered uniform for his personal effects. She found the task too much and broke down.

The senior chief told her it was OK to take a break, and my assistant Meyer and I took over the grim task of rummaging through the dead soldier's pockets. All his belongings were carefully catalogued and placed in a large zip-locked plastic bag. Meyer asked me if his family would be able to view his body, and I said since his head was intact, a good mortician could make him viewable.

Our senior chief, Meyer, and I rode to the mortuary in the back of the ambulance. On the gurney was the soldier's corpse enclosed in a flag-covered, black plastic body bag. The senior chief, a respiratory therapist who works in an ER in the civilian world, asked, "Did you notice that faint smell in casualty receiving?" We both said yes. "It's the smell of brains," he said. "It's not a strong odor, but once you smell it you never forget it." We didn't say anything in response.

Inside the mortuary, Meyer told the escort vehicle crew who had accompanied the ambulance to the morgue what would happen next. An escort vehicle with armed guards is required for ambulances traveling after dark in Kuwait. I noticed the shocked expressions on the faces of men who, for the first time, saw how the bodies were prepared for shipment home. I must have looked like that on my first visit here, too, I thought. Now I'm helping prepare them for what they are about to see.

The private's body was gently packed in bags of ice, the aluminum coffin sealed, and a large American flag reverently placed on it. He was now ready for his last trip home. At the senior chief's command we rendered a salute.

As we walked from the building I said to Meyer, "Anyone who would ever speak of war and glory in the same breath needs to spend an hour in that room."

My feelings at that moment were best captured in one of Studdert Kennedy's poems:

Waste

Waste of Muscle, waste of Brain,
Waste of Patience, waste of Pain,
Waste of Manhood, waste of Health,
Waste of Beauty, waste of Wealth,

Waste of Blood, and waste of Tears,
Waste of Youth's most precious years,
Waste of ways the Saints have trod,
Waste of Glory, waste of God—
    War!

Chapter 6

Hope Will Win Out

Today is the Sunday of Memorial Day weekend, and all day the flag of my adopted state of Rhode Island will fly over our hospital. The flag bears a symbol of the ancient church—a variation of the cross in the sign of an anchor. And the Ocean State's motto spells out the anchor's message—Hope. Hope is what I desperately need on this Memorial Day. Hope that one day human beings will set aside the madness of war and embrace peace. Hope that God will bring out of this horrible conflict a new day of justice, dignity, and freedom for the people of this region.

Yet I am spiritually conflicted on this Memorial Day, because I know that come September 11, I will fly the flag of my native Virginia from the same flagpole. Virginia's flag displays a victorious, bare-breasted Amazon

41

armed with a sword and spear with her foot firmly planted on the chest of a dead king. His crown is on the ground beside him and his hands hold the chains of slavery and the whip of oppression. Under his body are written the Commonwealth's motto: *Sic Semper Tyrannis*—Thus Always to Tyrants. And, sadly, as I know from my service at Pentagon recovery operations following the September 11 attacks in 2001, sometimes tyrants can only be defeated by force of arms.

As a Christian, I believe that one day, in God's time, hope will win out over war. As an American I pray that this war will end soon and that all who have died will not have died in vain. Memorial Day 2005 reminds me, once again, to give thanks to God for the brave men and women who worked for peace by giving their lives for us. I pray that our nation will always honor their memory by living the values of freedom, justice, human dignity, and peace that define our country at our best.

> That God can do no wrong is indeed the truest of all truth; but that does not mean that there is no wrong, but that wrong is against God's will, that He hates it, that it thwarts and tortures

Him, that He is constantly and actively striving to overcome it, and is overcoming it, and finally that He calls upon us, not for passive resignation, but for fierce and strenuous opposition in His Name.

God can do no wrong, Chaplain Studdert Kennedy, but we can when we take up arms, especially in the name of God. In 1918 your war's moral imperative seemed to be much clearer than my war's. Yet your "War to End All Wars" led to a greater war and to the Holocaust and Hiroshima. Where will our war lead?

Chapter 7

Have You Seen the Chaplain?

One Day in the Desert: 30 March, 2005

0545: I'm in the head looking in the mirror and scraping the hair off my face with a blue plastic razor. I have always hated getting up early and here I am, doing it again and again and again! My hair seems to be getting a little long and shaggy. It's at least a quarter of an inch long around the sides, so I'll have to visit the barber soon.

0615: Breakfast. The chow here is really great. Eggs any way you want 'em. Sausage and French toast, fresh fruit and grits are served every day. I eat breakfast with Petty Officer Meyer, my chaplain's assistant, and some other enlisted members of our unit. Nobody here complains about the food.

0700: Office admin time. I look at my email and Meyer checks on the religious census of the patients admitted since yesterday. I touch base with the commanding and executive officers.

0800: I talk with a chief petty officer about an unmarried female sailor in her department who has been reassigned due to the appearance of an "inappropriate relationship" with another sailor of the same rank who is married. I question the petty officer how she defines "appearance." She says the two sailors have been seen spending a lot of time together. I ask if anyone has actually seen any inappropriate displays between the two. She says no, but "their relationship doesn't look good." I mention two other sailors who have been an item since we were mobilized. She says the difference is that they're both single. I caution her about being too quick to hang a scarlet letter on someone. I promise to follow up with a talk with her sailor. I also wonder why she didn't reassign the male sailor.

0830: Petty Officer Meyer and I travel to the military dog kennel for the re-enlistment ceremony of Petty Officer Second Class Mruk.

She is an active duty master at arms, the Navy equivalent of an MP. PO Mruk has honored me by asking if I would re-enlist her. This is the first time in my career as a naval officer that I've done this. We go to the dog obstacle course and stand in front of a large stepped pyramid/bridge-shaped structure. Two army MPs climb half way up each side of it with their German shepherds. Mruk and I stand on the ground in front, facing each other. Her bomb-sniffing black lab Kato is sitting beside her. I look at the re-enlistment document I must sign. She was born in 1984 and is twenty-one. She has been in the Navy for four years and is re-enlisting for five more. She is proud of her work, loves her dog, and loves the Navy. I tell her I'm impressed that she has made second class in four years and I predict she'll be a master chief one day. She laughs and modestly says "Maybe, Sir."

I ask her to raise her right hand and repeat the oath after me. She swears to obey the orders of officers appointed over her and to defend this country "against all enemies, foreign and domestic. So help me God." I shake her hand and congratulate her on this solemn new commitment and tell her I'm proud of her. She represents the very best our country has—a young person who is courageous, loyal, idealistic, and patriotic. I pray that the results of this war will be worth the sacrifice of so many young men and women like her.

0900: We visit office work spaces of Naval Expeditionary Logistics Support Group— Forward Oscar, a customs inspection unit that is a part of my flock. We encounter a group of six senior NCOs in the passageway examining the scalp of one of their colleagues. I ask what is going on. Chief Smith, the examinee, proudly shows me the twenty-two stitches our hospital put in the back of her head yesterday. I ask what happened and she tells me that she was shaving her legs in the shower and slipped and fell. "I'm lucky that I'm a hard-headed Polack, Chaplain!" she says with a laugh. "We need bathtubs in the female barracks—can't you do anything about that, Sir? It's a safety issue!" Again, there is more laughter from everyone. I tell her, with a chuckle, that I'll look into it.

1130: I eat lunch next to a delightful command sergeant major who tells me about his twenty-eight years in the army. He says that he barely could read when he enlisted at seventeen. The military examined his eyes for the first time in his life and found he desperately needed glasses. He says, "Chaplain, it is wonderful to see, really see, for the first time in my life. All the time I was in school I thought that I was just dumb. My teachers did, too. Now I've got both associates and bachelors degrees, and I'm nine hours short of finishing my masters in business administration." The army was salvation for this impoverished kid from rural Georgia, and he has taken advantage of everything it offered to him.

1430: I meet with twenty-year-old Lance Corporal Honeycutt and his platoon sergeant, Staff Sergeant Fleeman. Honeycutt, a squared-away Marine who loves the Corps, wants to go home. His nineteen-year-old wife is seven months pregnant, and a civilian psychiatrist has diagnosed her as bipolar with panic attacks. She cannot take any medication due to her pregnancy (she had a miscarriage two years ago when they were first married). They have no other family members who can stay with her. His command has received a Red Cross message confirming this situation, and his commanding officer and first sergeant still refuse to let him go home. He is not a mission-essential person—his job consists of putting labels on boxes being shipped home to the states. I know the Marine Corps takes pride in its tradition of "Marines taking care of Marines," so I do two things. I fire off a stern email to his first sergeant and lieutenant colonel, and I get the kid an appointment tomorrow with one of our psychiatrists to review his wife's case. I cannot promise he'll go home. I do promise him that I'll fight to make the Marine Corps treat his wife and him fairly.

1530: I visit the wards and talk with an army specialist who took a shot through his upper thigh. Thankfully, the bullet did not hit the bone or major blood vessels. He's going back to his unit in Iraq tomorrow. He laughs and jokes about his "lucky" wound that missed the really important stuff nearby! His earthy gallows humor doubles me over in laughter.

1700: I'm caught outside at "colors." I'm on my way from the laundry to the mess hall for dinner. It is the custom on every military base that a bugle call is blown when the flag is lowered at the end of the day. Everyone outside stands at attention and salutes until the last note is sounded. I hold my salute and remember how important these simple rituals are to giving meaning and structure to my life over here.

1900: Lance Corporal Honeycutt calls me in a fit of fearful rage. His commanding officer has just called his wife and told her that he will not be coming home. She is in emotional melt-down. He begs me to call her in North Carolina and I do. I tell her about his appointment with the psychiatrist tomorrow, and that his colonel does not have that information yet. After about a half hour she is calmer and is willing to wait twenty-four hours to see what will happen. I call the lance corporal back and reassure him that she will wait twenty-four hours.

2000: I have a department head and chief petty officers' meeting with the commanding officer. The skipper passes us some information on his awards policy, on when we might go home, and about which unit will relieve us. There is nothing definite about our relief yet. He fields a few questions and, once again, I am reminded that the old adage that I used as a teacher—"There's no such thing as a stupid question"—is a lie.

2100: The chief's meeting with the command master chief (the senior enlisted person in the hospital, equal in rank to a command sergeant major in the army, and the commanding officer's right hand man). I am honored that the master chief has invited me to sit in. I suspect that he expects some "heavy swells" tonight. He is as tough and salty as a master chief can get, which is saying something. An Oklahoman, he is proud he is half American Indian. He retired as a lieutenant after twenty-two years on the Oklahoma City police department's vice squad. He is a relic of a Navy that is rapidly passing away, and this deployment is his last hurrah before he retires from the Navy next year. The meeting goes without a hitch.

2200: I revisit my desk before hitting my rack. The petty officer on watch says, "Hey Chaps, listen to this." Smiling, he hands me the phone. This man is a real character and I brace myself for what I think will probably be his latest scatological attempt to shock me. On the phone I hear a child's voice singing, "Twinkle, twinkle, little star..." It is his four-year-old daughter, back home in Texas, singing for her Daddy. I fight to hold back my tears and I thank him for sharing such a wonderful gift with me.

2300: Back in my rack. Since I am a senior officer, I have the rare luxury of not having someone in the upper bunk above my bed—for now. And in my seven-by-seven-foot living space I get two narrow wall lockers instead of one. I miss home and I thank God my days are so full, so that time seems to pass quickly.

Chapter 8

Lance Corporal Stein

Lance Corporal Stein is a Marine reservist who came to our hospital to have his knee injury repaired. He is a "grunt," an infantryman, whose unit was stationed in Iraq near the Syrian border as part of Operation Matador. They were tasked with hunting down and killing insurgents crossing the border. I received a call that he wanted to see the chaplain, so I hurried over. He had just read in the *Stars and Stripes* that four members of his platoon had been killed and about a dozen wounded in a firefight three days ago. All of the dead Marines were his friends. The *Stars and Stripes* said that his platoon "effectively ceased to exist" after the battle. He was overwhelmed with shock, grief, and guilt about not being there with them. He asked me if he could have a rabbi visit him and I had to tell him, sadly, that there was not a rabbi in Kuwait, but I would try to get the lay leader of our Jewish community to see him.

Two days later, while serving as the base duty chaplain, I received a call that Lance Corporal Stein wanted to see me. I met him at the chapel and he told me that he had just gotten a "Dear John" email from his fiancée. He was grieving the deaths of his friends, healing from leg surgery, and now his fiancée had told him she didn't want to marry him. We talked for an hour and a half. He told me he was twenty and a sophomore at Michigan State when he was recalled. He had joined the Marine Reserves after high school graduation to get money for college. His fiancée (age nineteen) had found someone else during the four months he was overseas. He believed she was just lonely, and she was now seeing a psychiatrist for depression. Stein also talked about how hard it was to practice his Jewish faith while living in the field. Finding meals that did not contain pork or shellfish products was difficult, and he would rinse his mouth with water from his canteen between eating meat and milk products. I admired this faithfulness and I wondered how many Episcopalians would be that dedicated in their religious discipline.

The young Marine said he did not think he could go back to Iraq because he "was tired of killing people." We talked some more and I realized that it was likely that he had post-traumatic stress disorder. So I asked him to agree to do the following:

1. Go to sick call tomorrow morning to be checked out by mental health.
2. Call his fiancée (I gave him a phone card) and talk to her in person about her health and the status of their relationship, because emails don't communicate as well as verbal conversation.
3. Attend the Friday evening Shabbat services at the chapel every week.

We talked again a week later. He had spoken to his fiancée, and they agreed to put their wedding plans on hold until she had gotten better and he had come home. He attended the Shabbat service, was warmly welcomed by his Jewish brothers and sisters, and planned to keep attending as long as he was at camp Arifjan. And he was diagnosed with post-traumatic stress disorder and treated by our mental health team.

Lance Corporal Stein did not have to go back to Iraq and kill more people. He was sent home to await a medical discharge. He plans to attend law school some day, yet he had to abandon his dream of being an active duty Marine Corps lawyer. He will, I pray, find a new dream.

Chapter 9

Who Goes to Heaven?

I'm continuing my conversation over here with the Reverend G. A. Studdert Kennedy, priest of the Church of England and the most famous chaplain of the British Army in World War I. His book, *The Hardest Part*, written about his experiences on the Western Front, inspires me to reflect theologically on my war. Here are his words on the occasion of the death of his chaplain's assistant.

> On the last Sunday in June, 1917 the Advanced Dressing Station in which I was working was blown in, and every one in it was killed except the doctor, two stretcher cases, a sergeant and myself. Among those killed was Roy Fergusson, my servant, a splendid lad of nineteen years, with whom I was great friends. He went out after the first shell had broken the end off the station to guide some of the walking wounded

to a place of safety and was killed instantly. I found him leaning against a heap of sandbags, his head buried in his hands, and a great hole in his back.

"Chaplain why don't you ever preach at the Contemporary Protestant service on Sunday mornings?" asked one of our enlisted people. My usual response is, "Because I officiate at the Episcopal eucharist on Saturdays at 1500." Today, Palm Sunday, I gave a different answer: "Because I believe in a God of infinite, unlimited grace. To preach that would make most of the people at that service angry and uncomfortable." I wanted to add, "And because many of them can't take a joke."

This Palm Sunday service was my final visit to the weekly "contemporary" service. Once again, I left it angry over the theological garbage that flowed from the pulpit. The preacher said, "The problem with America is that our people have abandoned their belief that the Bible is the unerring word of God. It says the only way to obtain forgiveness of our sins is through the shedding of blood. The only way to atone for sin was that God had to let his Son suffer and die. You must believe and accept Jesus Christ as your Lord and Savior before you die or you are lost forever. If you haven't done this, don't wait. Now is the time. You could die tonight, unsaved."

That afternoon I had lunch with two of our physicians. One is a second-generation American of Japanese ancestry and a self-described "Shinto-Roman Catholic." The other is a second-generation Indian-American and a practicing Hindu. We spent forty-five minutes discussing the nature of God. I realized once again that the God of the fundamentalist preacher isn't as lovable or as loving as are many of the gods we talked about at lunch. What sane, thinking person would worship the "Contemporary Protestant" chaplain's God? His God requires an unquestioning belief in every word of a book which describes a blood-thirsty deity who is also an abusive parent. His God required the suffering and death of his only child in order finally to forgive his own flawed creation. His is a God who consigns people to hell if they don't say they believe in his Son before they die. One second after you take your last breath is too late, and there you are in torment for eternity. It is the old "turn or burn" theology that has frightened people into belief for centuries. I believe such a God is unfit for human worship because many human beings are more kind, forgiving, and loving than that chaplain's God. I was at lunch with two of these compassionate folks today. I can't imagine a God who reaches out his arms of love on the cross as ever losing either one of these men. This war and this place reaffirm my need to believe in a God with a human face who knows the brokenness and pain of the human condition from the inside out.

The God of the sermon I heard today is as far from the God I love, serve, and worship as I can imagine. My God created the universe and succumbed to all the evil that creation could dish out: my God was crucified and died on Good Friday. The phrase "Son of God" is shorthand for "God from God, Light from Light, true God from true God…of one Being with the Father. Through him all things were made." My dying God overcame death itself, and he gives us not just life after death, but life after birth, here and now, through his love for us. Knowing this, one cannot help but love

God in return. And I believe that God, in Jesus the Christ, will one day redeem everything and everyone he has made through his self-giving love.

> Roy was a fine Christian. What about men who aren't? There are many men who die fine deaths who have no faith, or at least no conscious faith, in God or Christ as Son of God. How about them? Well, God is greater than the Churches. He is the source and the only source, of all fine life of the spirit. If a man dies for duty's sake a death which is for his spirit not defeat but victory, he dies in Christ. That is how it looks to me. Christ is the Lord of all good life. He is the only source of splendid life of the spirit which turns defeat in death to victory. This gift of the "life eternal" is indeed poured out upon me through the Church and the appointed means of grace, but we cannot confine God to His covenants. The river of eternal life breaks through a thousand channels and finds the soul of man.

I find it hard to understand how any chaplain over here could hold a narrow view of God. How can a chaplain miss the truth that there are "a thousand channels" of "the river of

eternal life," and human beings "cannot con-
fine God to His covenants?" We military
clergy minister to many folks who are going
into and coming out of combat "up north."
Many are broken and crippled physically, emotionally, and spiritually by this war. Scaring
already frightened soldiers into faith is not true
to the spirit of Jesus. And far too often these
same pastors also lack the surest sign of God's
presence, the ability to laugh: at the military,
their country, their religion, and themselves.
They forget, or maybe never knew, the great
truth that joy marked by laughter is a certain
sign of the kingdom of God. In the Easter lit-
urgy of the Orthodox Church the priest says
to the congregation, "Alleluia, Christ is risen."
The people respond: "The Lord is risen in-
deed, alleluia." And then the priest says, "Now
let us laugh," and the congregation celebrates
the resurrection by laughing together out loud
for a few minutes. There is healing in laughter,
especially in the grimmest, saddest, most God-
awful situations. And the devil always loves it
when we are "dead serious" (isn't that a mar-
velously descriptive term)—especially when
we take ourselves too seriously.

My fundamentalist chaplain colleagues will be surprised one day when they see firsthand that "great multitude that no one could count, from every nation, from all tribes, and peoples and languages, standing before the throne and before the Lamb, robed in white, with palm branches in their hands" (Revelation 7:9), for among this "multitude" will be all those folks they knew with certainty would never be acceptable to God. I plan to be there in that motley crew, partying away. And I'll echo our Lord's welcome to my fundamentalist colleagues to join all of us sinners who'll be laughing at death at the great feast of the Lamb.

> My friends have been grieved because I made jokes about serious subjects and serious people. In such matters one should be dead serious I have been told. This is a point of view which is difficult for an Irishman to understand at any time, but is doubly difficult for one who has served with the armies at the front. Out here making fun is the most serious business of our lives. I doubt if it is possible, and I am sure it is not wholesome for any living man to be dead serious. To lack a sense of humor is one of the

most terrible handicaps in life for anyone, and it is a disaster in a writer or a preacher who wants to help. I have made fun of the Archbishop of Canterbury, but I firmly believe he is one of the brightest and best people in England. Christian laughter always hovers just on the brink of tears, for God in Christ has redeemed them both and wedded joy to sorrow, and real peace to pain.

Amen, Chaplain Studdert Kennedy.

Chapter 10

The Cost of Freedom

Our casualty receiving team was lined up at the helipad wearing helmets and preparing a gurney. "What's up?" I asked. "We're getting a bad one in from up north, Sir," the leading petty officer replied. A medevac helicopter was inbound from Bukka, Iraq, and was expected within five minutes. The casualty had been in the turret of an overturned gun truck—an up-armored humvee with a .50 caliber machine gun on top. We did not know if the cause was a pothole, an IED, driving too fast, or a traffic accident—it didn't matter to our staff. What we did know was that the patient had a left arm almost completely severed at the shoulder, had arrested in the helo and was receiving CPR enroute, and had extensive facial injuries rendering him almost unrecognizable. We were his only hope because we were the only hospital nearby with a vascular surgeon on staff.

The helicopter arrived and the team went to work. As the door with its giant red cross painted on a white square slid open we could see a crewman pumping away on our casualty's chest while another medic squeezed air into his lungs through a plastic bag. The injured soldier was gently lifted from the helo and rushed into our CASREC tent as the helo's medic rode on top of the gurney, all the while continuing chest compressions.

Our docs, nurses, and corpsmen soon got the soldier's heart beating again, and I was asked to tell the aircrew medic that his patient now had a pulse. The young sergeant who had worked so hard in the air to save him wept openly at this news. Yet things were worse than we expected.

The patient was Private First Class Andrew Mitchell, aged twenty-one, from a small town in Arkansas. No one expected him to survive because both eye orbits were shattered and he would probably lose his sight; his lower jaw was broken in several places; his upper jaw was broken away from his skull; his nose was torn almost completely away from his face; the right side of his face was filleted with an open six-inch gash down to the fragments of his jawbone; his left arm was virtually detached at the shoulder with a near-severed brachial artery—and there was no room to place a tourniquet (which meant that, in spite of the pressure applied to his arm by medics in Iraq, Andrew had experienced a critical loss of blood). He would almost certainly lose his arm. No one knew what damage had been done to his brain, neck, and belly. CASREC gave him blood, put him on a ventilator, and rushed him into the O.R. to repair his torn blood vessels.

I was told to stand by to give him last rites. Our anesthesiologist talked to me about his chances as they wheeled him out of casualty receiving. "He's got the 'disease' of being twenty-one and the strong heart that goes with it. Guys our age would have never survived the medevac. Odds are overwhelming he will not come out of the O.R. alive."

"Chaplain, I don't want to go to the APOD again," said a corpsman watching from the passageway. "Aerial Port of Debarkation" is the military name for the section of Kuwait International Airport where units deploying to Kuwait and Iraq enter this theatre. It is also the site of the morgue where those who die over here exit. This petty officer had been on more than one mortuary detail with me. All I could say was, "Petty Officer MacCawley, I'm sorry, but it looks like we're going to do that again tonight—and we'll be OK."

I ran to get my oil stock, my purple and white stole, and my pocket-sized *A Prayer Book for the Armed Forces*. The sailors who work in admin always know things aren't looking good when I run to my desk and grab those items. My next stop was Patient Admin (PAD). I asked if they had a faith group identity on the private. It is critical to know the patient's religion. While almost any chaplain is received gratefully by an injured soldier, in grave condition it matters whether a person is Protestant, Orthodox, Anglican, Roman Catholic, Jewish, or of some other faith in order to provide the prayers and ministry of his own faith group. Mitchell did not have dog tags with him. They were probably removed at the field hospital in Iraq. We did have his ID card. I looked at the handsome young face staring back at me from the small piece of plastic in my hand. PAD did a quick inquiry to his unit and determined he was Baptist, so I was able to be his pastor. The data search also revealed other information: he was married just prior to deployment, to another soldier. His wife, also twenty-one, was stationed in Louisiana. She was three months pregnant.

CASREC quickly handed Andrew off to the O.R. team. I stood with the chief of nursing services in the pre-op/post-op tent and we watched the work through the clear plastic strips that separated us from the operating room. PFC Mitchell's heart arrested again and we saw someone begin chest compressions. I thumbed through the Prayer Book and steadied myself for the inevitable invitation to enter the O.R. to commend Private First Class Andrew Mitchell into the "arms of God's mercy, into the blessed rest of everlasting peace, and into the glorious company of the saints in light."

The television was on in post-op. Fox News announced the Iraqi government was still hashing out their new constitution. They finally seemed to agree on the name for the new nation: The Federal Republic of Iraq. The news was a dissonant counterpoint to the drama playing out before our eyes. I had always believed freedom was not free. The man on the table was paying this price with his life in front of me. Our magnificently talented docs, nurses, and corpsmen were giving a part of their lives to save him. "Is this the cost of freedom?" I wondered. "Do those in the Iraqi parliament know what this is costing? Are they grateful for the opportunity for a better world that PFC Mitchell has given them with his life? Do they care?"

Fifteen minutes later Mitchell had a pulse. During the next two and a half hours the O.R. techs had us run errands to the lab and pharmacy to ferry blood and medications to their team. Twenty units of blood went into his body in the three hours he was in surgery. As she searched for the right sized suturing silk, one O.R. nurse said, "It's easier for me to work on somebody without a face—I can detach because he is less human, less personal."

Finally they were done and he was moved to ICU. The oral surgeons had stabilized his facial bones so that an airway would remain open. Andrew's head was totally wrapped in an Ace bandage. He looked like a basketball with a breathing tube sticking out. The vascular surgeon had grafted new arteries and the orthopedic surgeon had pinned the bones in his left arm. Now it was time to wait twenty-four hours. No one expected him to live through the night.

A vigil was kept for Andrew Mitchell overnight in our makeshift ICU. I slept fitfully that night waiting for my cell phone to ring with a summons to pray at his bedside as he died. As the sun rose, we were all surprised that he was still very much alive, and making urine.

On the second day Andrew was taken to radiology for a CT scan, and neck and spinal x-rays. Miraculously, his brain had no bleeds and his neck and backbone were intact. He returned to surgery that afternoon, to further stabilize his broken face and to prepare him for a flight to the larger military hospital at Landstuhl, Germany, and from there on to Walter Reed. I was amazed to see him when he returned to the ICU. He now had a face that looked like a face. Surgeons said he had circulation again in his left arm, and he might not lose it. The prognosis was that the limb would be immobile and withered, but he would keep the arm. His eyesight was still a toss-up. The docs couldn't check his pupils due to the powerful sedatives he was taking. And they still weren't sure how the loss of blood affected his brain. But he was alive, and he had beaten all the odds, and he was going home.

At 0415 today, as a pink and purple mackerel sky dawned, we wheeled PFC Andrew Mitchell out to a waiting helicopter. We paused for a moment for a prayer before the litter team placed him on the medevac. I thanked God for those in our hospital who gave so selflessly and heroically of themselves to get Andrew to this moment, and I prayed that six months from now he would know the joy of holding his new baby in his arms.

Pray for peace.

Chapter 11

Coincidences and Karaoke

Not every experience in war is a frightening, life-or-death one. Surviving the life-or-death moments is possible because of the seemingly little, inconsequential things that humanize a military outpost, help a soldier relax, and make home seem not quite so far away. Just meeting someone who roots for your baseball team, is acquainted with a friend or teacher of yours, or has visited your home town can make a huge difference.

The very first patient I visited in our hospital was an Air Guardsman from Charlestown, Rhode Island. He asked me where I was from and when I told him, he said with disdain, "Oh, Barrington!" I told him that contrary to the prevailing stereotype, not everyone in our lovely town was an elitist snob, and that there were actually many nice people there. He was a lifelong citizen of the Ocean State, but I didn't ask if he'd ever visited Barrington. I'd lived in Rhode Island long enough to know how insurmountable the fifteen-mile distance is from the West to the East Bay.

I was later at the bedside of a young infantry soldier who had come down from Iraq to have his broken ankle repaired. He mentioned that his grandfather who died in December had been a priest. "Episcopal?" I asked. "Yes, Episcopal," he replied. I told him I was an Episcopal priest and asked his grandfather's name. "Thom Blair."

"Was he rector of Trinity Church, Boston?"

"Yes, did you know him, Chaplain?"

I said I might have met him once, but I felt I knew him because for three years I saw his picture every day on the wall of my church's parish hall. He and I had served the same rural congregation, Immanuel Church, in the village of Old Church in Hanover County, Virginia. His grandfather was rector in 1948 and 1949 and I was rector from 1981 to 1984. I then told the soldier that his uncle, also named Thom Blair, and I were friends from our days in the Diocese of Virginia. Thom the Younger had retired the year before and his nephew said he had moved to Kilmarnock, Virginia, where he was building a house. I told him to give his "Uncle Tommy" my very best.

A young Marine lance corporal asked to see me. I asked the standard questions about his unit, military job, active or reserve status, hometown, and family. He was a "grunt," an infantryman on his third tour to Iraq, and in our hospital for knee surgery. He had joined the Corps at seventeen and had just turned twenty. He was single and his hometown was Fredericksburg, Virginia. I told him I grew up in Culpeper, just thirty miles up the road. His face lit up when we began talking about life in Virginia. I asked him if Carl's Ice Cream on Princess Anne Street was still in business. He said yes and we both agreed that Carl's had the best soft-serve ice cream in the world. When I asked him what was on his mind he said he was having trouble sleeping, and he showed me his left hand which had a slight tremor. I asked if he'd seen much combat and he said that he had. "I don't have any trouble killing people, Sir. If I didn't kill them they'd kill me. But I don't want to kill any more children. Insurgents often use them as shields when they attack us, knowing we will hesitate to shoot back. But we don't hesitate. And the children are usually afraid and crying because the kids know what they are being used for, and that they are going to die. At other times kids just get in the way of our ordnance and we unintentionally kill them. I can't get their faces out of my mind."

I told him he was probably dealing with PTSD (post-traumatic stress disorder—the "shell shock" or "battle fatigue" of previous wars) and that I would walk with him over to the mental health clinic. I turned him over to one of our psychiatrists. A week later he walked into my office. He extended his hand and thanked me for what I'd done for him. He said he was looking forward to getting back to his unit in Iraq; he was sleeping all night now; his tremors had stopped; and he felt better than he had in weeks. We agreed that after the war, the first one of us to get back to Fredericksburg would have a dish of Carl's ice cream and think of the other guy.

Another thing that helps soldiers survive is the distraction and laughter which entertainment provides. When well-known actors and musicians visit the front, soldiers know they are not forgotten, but often the entertainment is generated among the troops themselves, and that is sometimes the best entertainment of all.

Karaoke Night was Thursday at our community center, and, yes, one can have karaoke without copious amounts of alcohol (it is illegal in Kuwait). And there is some real talent over here. One guy sang "War Pigs," and sounded just like Ozzy Osbourne. Twenty minutes later he did a credible job as Bobby Darin on "Mack the Knife." Our civilian Filipino DJ and host took the microphone for a hilarious rendition of Will Smith's "Get Jiggy with It." One young soldier with a beautiful tenor voice sang "Butterfly Kisses" (the most popular wedding reception song ever), and there was hardly a dry eye in the place (except mine—this old cynic has gagged over that saccharine song for years). Two young women sang a duet of a Reba McEntire song and harmonized wonderfully. They had real talent. I'll look out for those two soldiers after the war when they hit the big time in Nashville. But the show stopper of the evening was a GI, a dead ringer for Shaquille O'Neal. He had everybody in the community center singing, clapping, and stomping their feet to Queen's classic "Fat Bottomed Girls." I'm sure the late, great, Freddie Mercury was laughing with us in rock and roll heaven as we sang:

> Oh, won't you take me home tonight?
> Oh, down beside your red firelight,
> Oh, and you give it all you got
> Fat bottomed girls, you make
>   the rockin' world go round."

Chapter 12

The Last Casualty

"Get ready, Chaplain, we've got a bad one coming in," the XO called as she rushed past my desk. I grabbed my small purple and white stole, holy oil, and a small armed forces prayer book and hurried to the patient administration office to find out what was going on. Patient admin was the heartbeat and the crossroads of our hospital. Its people were often the unsung heroes of our mission. They made connections getting people into and out of Iraq, and on to Landstuhl, Germany. The radios used to communicate with the medevac helicopters were also located in their tent.

"What's going on?" I asked the admin chief.

"A humvee got hit by an IED just north of the border. Two personnel were killed, one Air Force and one Army. We've got the surviving

Army guy inbound. They should be here in twenty minutes." Soon I heard the familiar sound of helicopter rotors approaching from the north.

The casualty receiving team brought Sergeant Andy Rivera in. They quickly found that his wounds were probably not mortal, but he was seriously injured. He had been in the turret when the bomb went off. His right femur was exposed and broken in six places; he had lost a testicle; and he had shrapnel wounds throughout his lower torso. He was still conscious when they wheeled him in. His best friend, who was riding in the same convoy, had come with him in the Blackhawk. I sat with this friend, Specialist Warren, as we waited for our medical team to work another miracle.

The soldiers were from a Texas National Guard unit and had been in the theatre for nine months. The convoy was carrying supplies from Kuwait to Baghdad, and they were ten miles into Iraq when they were attacked. The soldier who was killed in the blast was a good friend of both Sergeant Rivera and the young man seated next to me. I reassured the frightened, grieving kid that we were the best combat support hospital in the region and that our doctors were tops in their specialties, with many years of experience in the civilian world.

Several hours later Andy was moved to our ICU and we went back to see him. He was conscious and alert. His broken leg was secured and immobilized in a metal framework, and he had a tube in his nose. The shrapnel taken from his body was in an amber colored plastic pill bottle and the young Texan said it sounded like a rattlesnake rattle when he shook it. One of our corpsmen told Sergeant Rivera that there were companies in the U.S. which took the shrapnel from wounded soldiers and turned it into jewelry for their wives and sweethearts. Andy said he didn't think his wife would want something like that and he was anxious to speak to her. He was thirty-two years old and had three kids, all under ten. I asked if he was a religious man and he said that he attended his Methodist Church in Waco every Sunday. All three of us held hands; I prayed for strength and healing for him and I thanked God he was alive.

His commanding officer arrived the next day. The captain, a field artilleryman, looked like he had stepped out of a recruiting poster. He was a huge, handsome, tough-looking black man who wore master parachutist wings and a Ranger tab on his uniform. He told Sgt. Rivera that he was praying for him, and he never stopped holding his hand the entire hour he was by his bed. Rivera would be sent to Landstuhl early the next morning, so this was a time to say good-bye. The captain offered some macho words: "Stay strong and we'll see you back in Texas. You're going to be there with us when we get off the plane, right?"

"Hooah, Sir!" Rivera replied.

The captain leaned over the bed and with tears in his eyes tenderly kissed the soldier's forehead.

I awoke at 3:30 the next morning to see him off. There were five patients on their way to Germany that day, four walking wounded, and Andy. We lined up outside in the darkness as the sounds of the rotors grew loud in the distance. "Is there anything I can do for you, Sergeant?" I asked. "Pray for me, Chaplain, I don't like helicopters much," he said with a smile. I held his hand and prayed for God's protection on the journey, for healing, and for peace.

The helo dropped from the sky with a roar and a cloud of dust. I could see the white squares with their red crosses in the lights of the helipad. The four ambulatory patients preceded him into the aircraft. He would be loaded last (the most critical cases are boarded last, so they can be off-loaded first). I walked behind his gurney and it felt good to follow a live patient after walking behind too many body bags. "It's great to walk behind someone who's gonna make it," I thought.

One more handshake. "I hope to see you in Texas one day, Sergeant."

"I hope you're not in my custody, Sir!" he replied. Rivera was a police officer in his civilian life. We both roared with laughter.

He was the last on. The door slid shut. I stood beside the surgeon who looked on with pride in his work. "God bless these medical people," I said to myself. "They have given so much of themselves this past year to make this sad and broken world a better place."

The rotors spun faster and the pilot pulled up, the blades clawing the air as the bird lifted off into the cool September night. We turned our backs to shield our eyes from the stinging sand and then turned and watched as the helicopter's lights disappeared into the darkness.

"Is there anything I can do for you, Andy?" I had asked a few minutes earlier. You don't know it, Sergeant Andrew Rivera, but by simply surviving you have done your very best for us. Thank you for living and giving me hope.

Chapter 13

After and Since:
Clutching for Hope

I know that the Cross is followed by an empty
tomb and victory. God is limited now, and has
been ever since creation began, by the necessities
inherent in His task; but those necessities
are not eternal, they are only temporary and
contingent, and God will overcome them in
the end. That is our faith.

The supreme strength of the Christian faith
is that it faces the foulest and filthiest of life's
facts in the crude brutality of the Cross, and
through them sees the Glory of God in Jesus
Christ. The vision of a Suffering God, revealed
in Jesus Christ, is a necessary Truth. Religion
is impossible when we try to go without or go
beyond the Incarnation (God becoming fully
human in Christ).

God never wills, nor can will, evil to anyone, anywhere, at any time. God is, has been, and always will be, pure undiluted, unmitigated Beauty, Goodness, and Truth—Infinite Love. Nothing in the world must make you compromise about that. You cannot live, and you cannot think rightly, until you grasp that and hold tightly to it. That is the truth which you have to hold by force of faith in the teeth of doubt, steadfastly denying whatever appears to contradict it, denying the world's denial of God's love.

War is the world's ultimate denial of God's love.

William Temple, Archbishop of Canterbury and Studdert Kennedy's friend, described him this way, "If to be a priest is to carry others on the heart and offer them with self in the sacrifice of human nature—the Body and the Blood—to God the Father of our Lord Jesus Christ, then Geoffrey Studdert Kennedy was the finest priest that I have known. To him the supreme consolation was found in the thought that God suffers. For him the great illumination came from the realization that God does not watch our sufferings from afar, but suffers in and with his children."

Who will separate us from the love of Christ? Will hardship, or distress, or persecution, or famine, or nakedness, or peril, or sword? No, in all these things we are more than conquerors through him who loved us. For I am convinced that neither death, nor life, nor angels, nor rulers, nor things present, nor things to come, nor powers, nor height, nor depth, nor anything else in all creation will be able to separate us from the love of God in Christ Jesus our Lord.

—Romans 8:35, 37-39

My year in that combat support hospital taught me to agree with Woodbine Willie. I cannot believe in God who does not suffer with us and for us. I need the cross and the crucifix. They bring me comfort and hope through our infinitely loving God who knows the human experience from the inside out. God is not only with us, he is one of us. I saw the crucified One in those courageous, broken soldiers who came to our hospital. I saw the hope of the resurrected Christ in the selfless service of our staff who worked for life and healing in the shadow of war and death.

High and Lifted Up

SEATED on the throne of power
    with the sceptre in Thine hand,
While a host of eager angels
    ready for Thy Service stand.
So it was the prophet saw Thee,
    in his agony of prayer,
While the sound of many waters
    swelled in music on the air,
Swelled until it burst like thunder
    in a shout of perfect praise,
"Holy, Holy, Holy Father,
    Potentate of years and days.
Thine the Kingdom, Thine the glory,
    Thine the splendour of the sun,
Thine the wisdom, Thine the honour,
    Thine the crown of victory won."

So it was the prophet saw Thee,
    so this artist saw Thee too,
Flung his vision into colour,
    mystery of gold and blue.

But I stand in woe and wonder;
      God, my God, I cannot see,
Darkness deep and deeper darkness—
      all the world is dark to me.
Where is power? Where is glory?
      Where is any victory won?
Where is wisdom? Where is honour?
      Where the splendour of the sun?
God, I hate this splendid vision—
      all its splendour is a lie,
Splendid fools see splendid folly,
      splendid mirage born to die.
As imaginary waters
      to an agony of thirst,
As the vision of a banquet
      to a body hunger-cursed,
As the thought of anaesthetic
      to a soldier mad with pain,
While his torn and tortured body
      turns and twists and writhes again,
So this splendid lying vision
      turns within my doubting heart,
Like a bit of rusty bayonet
      in a torn and festering part.

Preachers give it me for comfort,
      and I curse them to their face,
Puny, petty-minded priestlings
      prate to me of power and grace;
Prate of power and boundless wisdom
      that takes count of little birds,
Sentimental poisoned sugar
      in a sickening stream of words.
Platitudinously pious
      far beyond all doubts and fears,
They will patter of God's mercy
      that can wipe away our tears.
All their speech is drowned in sobbing,
      and I hear the great world groan,
As I see a million mothers
      sitting weeping all alone,
See a host of English maidens
      making pictures in the fire,
While a host of broken bodies
      quiver still on German wire.
And I hate the God of Power
      on His hellish heavenly throne,
Looking down on rape and murder,
      hearing little children moan.
Though a million angels hail Thee
      King of Kings, yet cannot I.

There is nought can break the silence
        of my sorrow save the cry,
"Thou who rul'st this world of sinners
        with Thy heavy iron rod,
Was there ever any sinner
        who has sinned the sin of God?
Was there ever any dastard who would
        stand and watch a Hun
Ram his bayonet through the bowels
        of a baby just for fun?
Praise to God in Heaven's highest
        and in all the depths be praise,
Who in all His works is brutal,
        like a beast in all His ways."

God, the God I love and worship,
        reigns in sorrow on the Tree,
Broken, bleeding, but unconquered,
        very God of God to me.
All that showy pomp of splendour,
        all that sheen of angel wings,
Was but borrowed from the baubles
        that surround our earthly kings.
Thought is weak and speech is weaker,
        and the vision that He sees

Strikes with dumbness any preacher,
        brings him humbly to his knees.
But the word that Thou hast spoken
        borrows nought from kings
        and thrones,
Vain to rack a royal palace
        for the echo of Thy tones.
In a manger, in a cottage,
        in an honest workman's shed,
In the homes of humble peasants,
        and the simple lives they led,
In the life of one an outcast
        and a vagabond on earth,
In the common things He valued,
        and proclaimed of priceless worth,
And above all in the horror
        of the cruel death He died,
Thou hast bid us seek Thy glory,
        in a criminal crucified.
And we find it—for Thy glory
        is the glory of Love's loss,
And Thou hast no other splendour
        but the splendour of the Cross.
For in Christ I see the martyrs
        and the beauty of their pain,

And in Him I hear the promise
      that my dead shall rise again.
High and lifted up, I see Him
      on the eternal Calvary,
And two pierced hands are stretching
      east and west o'er land and sea.
On my knees I fall and worship
      that great Cross that shines above,
For the very God of Heaven
      is not Power, but Power of Love.

FROM *The Unutterable Beauty:*
The Collected Poetry of
G. A. Studdert Kennedy